STORIES
And
SONGS
Of
JESUS

STORIES
And
SONGS
Of
JESUS

Paule Freeburg, D.C.
Christopher Walker
Illustrated by
Jean Germano

OCP PUBLICATIONS

This Book Belongs To

Stories And Songs Of Jesus
© 1994, OCP Publications
5536 NE Hassalo
Portland, OR 97213 U.S.A.

Music and text © 1994, Christopher Walker and Paule Freeburg, DC
Illustrations © 1994, Jean Germano
Published by OCP Publications
All rights reserved

CREDITS:

Publisher — *John J. Limb*
Executive Editor — *Paulette Vaught*
Managing Editor — *Joanne Osborn*
Project Editor — *Craig Kingsbury*
Editing Assistance — *Mary Straub, Luciana Powell, James A. Wilde*
Music Engraving — *Sharon Norton, director; Laura Wasson*
Graphic Assistance — *Ralph Sanders*
Art Director — *Jean Germano*

Stories And Songs Of Jesus
Book .... edition 9404
Stereo Cassette .... edition 9405
Activity/Coloring Book .... edition 10019

Edition 9404
ISBN 0-915531-27-5

Printed in Mexico
Third Printing 2001
(RRDR 0701)

Introduction

Dear Children

You are holding a book that will tell you about the most wonderful person in the world. Although he lived on the earth long ago, we believe he is still with us to help us. His name is Jesus and we hope you will become friends with him as we are.

In this book you will hear many things about Jesus: how he helped people who were hurt, sick or in trouble. Jesus used to tell stories to show us how to be loving to one another.

With each story you will find a song to sing about how Jesus helps us and wants to be our friend. We hope that as you hear the stories and sing the songs, you will want to talk with Jesus and tell him all that happens to you! He will always listen, whether you are sad or happy. Remember, he will always be your friend.

Yours in the love of Jesus,
Chris and Paule

Dear Grownups

Wearied by the stresses of life, many of us sigh, "Oh, to be a child again." Psychologists encourage us to "re-discover the child within." When the disciples of Jesus, eager to protect his schedule, wanted to keep children away, Jesus startled them by saying, "Unless you become like these children, you will not enter God's heavenly reign." What is so special about 'being a child'? What did Jesus want us to learn from children about how we relate with him? Perhaps it is their wide-eyed wonder at life with its beauty, challenge and newness. Or maybe it is their openness, their acceptance of the probable and the not so probable. It might be their joy in simple things. All these point to the sparks of divinity in us that Jesus can speak to most freely.

We hope that you parents, godparents, brothers and sisters, aunts, uncles, grandparents and teachers will read these Stories And Songs Of Jesus to children and find your own faith nourished as you share them. We hope that in singing these songs your children celebrate their love of Jesus and his love for them. The gospel stories are written simply, in children's language to keep the good news alive in their hearts.

Both of our childhoods were graced with the sharing of God's word and we were called into a relationship with the Lord Jesus through the Scriptures. Working together we often recalled in ourselves a truth of Jesus that took root when we were children. It is our desire that children for whom Stories And Songs Of Jesus has been written will come to know the Lord's love in their own hearts and celebrate that love with their lives.

Yours in the love of Jesus,
Paule and Chris

Table of Contents

Table of Contents

An Angel Came From Heaven

A long, long time ago in the town of Nazareth, there was a man called Joseph and a woman called Mary. Mary and Joseph loved each other very much and they were going to get married.

One day God sent the angel Gabriel to visit Mary and to tell her something very special. Gabriel said, "Rejoice Mary, God loves you very much. You are going to have a baby, and you will name him Jesus, because he will save his people."

Mary didn't understand what the angel was telling her. So she asked Gabriel, "How can I have a baby now? Joseph and I aren't married yet." The angel Gabriel said, "The power of the Holy Spirit will make this happen. Your baby will be holy, and he will be called the Son of God."

Mary said to the angel, "I believe God loves me very much. Yes, I will do whatever God wants me to do." Then the Angel Gabriel went back to heaven.

Glory To God

1. Glo - ry, glo - ry to God, __ glo - ry,
2. Peace to peo - ple on earth, __ peace to
3. An - gels sing of the Lord, __ an - gels
4. Shep - herds wor - ship the Lord, __ shep - herds
5. We've seen Je - sus the Lord, __ we've seen
6. Kings bring gifts to the Lord, __ kings bring
7. Now we come to the Lord, __ now we

1. glo - ry to God, ___ in the high - est heav - en
2. peo - ple on earth, ___ in the high - est heav - en
3. sing of the Lord ___ in the high - est heav - en
4. wor - ship the Lord ___ and sing joy - ful prais - es
5. Je - sus the Lord ___ and sing joy - ful prais - es
6. gifts to the Lord, ___ and sing joy - ful prais - es
7. come to the Lord, ___ and sing joy - ful prais - es

1-6
1.-6. glo - ry, glo - ry to God. _____

Final
7. God. _____ Glo - ry to

7. God. ___ Glo - ry to God. _____

Once there was a man called Joseph and his wife, Mary. They lived in the town of Nazareth. One day, the ruler of their country made a new law. He said, "I want everyone to go to the town where they were born to sign a book so that I will know how many people live in my country."

So Mary and Joseph went to the town of Bethlehem, because that was where Joseph's family came from. It was a long way to go, and it was very hard for Mary because she was going to have a baby.

When Joseph and Mary got to Bethlehem, they looked for somewhere to stay. But there were so many people in Bethlehem, they couldn't find a room anywhere. They looked and they looked, and they looked until it was night. But the only place they could find was in a stable, where the animals lived. Mary and Joseph were so tired, they stayed right there. And during the night, there in the stable, Mary had her baby, who was Jesus. She wrapped the baby in a blanket and laid him in a manger because there was no room for them anywhere else.

In the fields near Bethlehem, there were shepherds, who were taking care of their sheep. Suddenly, in the middle of the night, an angel of God came to them and there was a bright light in the sky. The shepherds were very frightened. So the angel said to them, "Don't be afraid. Listen, I am bringing good news for you and for everyone! A baby boy was born tonight in Bethlehem. He is the Savior, Jesus the Lord. He has come to bring peace and joy to all people."

Suddenly there were angels all over the sky, praising God and singing, "Glory to God, glory to God in heaven. Peace on earth to all people."

Then the angels went back to heaven. The shepherds were so excited they said, "Let's go and see this new baby." So they hurried away to the town of Bethlehem. And when they found the stable, they saw Mary and Joseph, and the baby Jesus lying in the manger. The shepherds were very happy to see them, and they told them what the angel had said about Jesus. Then the shepherds went back to the fields, praising

God, saying, "We have seen the Savior, Jesus the Lord."

Later, three wise men came from the East. They were following a beautiful, bright star. The star led them to Bethlehem and stopped right over the stable where Jesus was. The three wise men went into the stable and they saw the baby with his mother Mary. They knelt in front of Jesus and treated him like a king. Then they gave him wonderful gifts. One brought gold, one brought frankincense and one brought myrrh. The next day, the three wise men went back to their own countries. And Mary remembered all these wonderful things that had happened and kept them in her heart.

Yes, We Will Do What Jesus Says

One day, two friends of Jesus were getting married. The wedding was in the town of Cana. It was not too far from where Jesus lived and so he went to the wedding with some of his friends and his mother Mary.

After the wedding, there was a big party and everyone stayed to celebrate with the bride and groom. During the party, Mary saw that there wasn't enough wine for everyone. So she said to her son Jesus, "There isn't any wine left. Will you help?" Jesus said, "It isn't time yet for me to do a miracle." But Mary knew he would help, so she said to the people who were serving the wine, "Just do whatever Jesus tells you to do."

Jesus said to the servers, "You see those big water jars over there?" When they looked, they saw six water jars, and they were very, very big. Jesus said, "Go and fill them all with water." So they went and filled the jars with water right to the top. Then Jesus said, "Now take some of the water out of the jars and let the people in charge taste it."

And what do you think happened when they tasted it? It wasn't water anymore. It was wine. Jesus had turned the water into wine. So now there was enough wine for everyone at the party.

This was the first miracle that Jesus ever did. He turned water into wine at a wedding party in the town of Cana.

Fishing For People

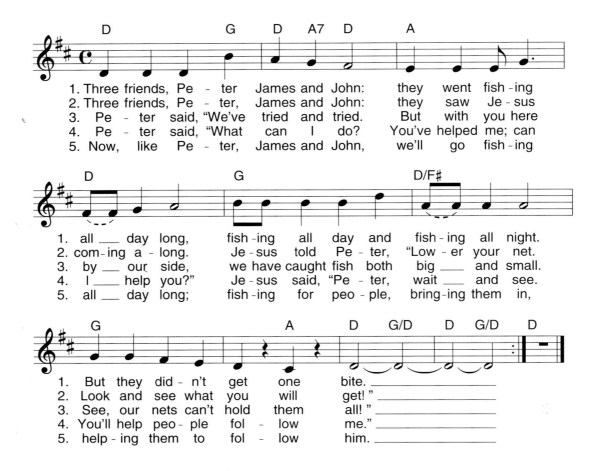

	D			G	D	A7	D		A	
1.	Three	friends, Pe – ter	James and John:	they	went	fish – ing
2.	Three	friends, Pe – ter,	James and John:	they	saw	Je – sus
3.	Pe – ter	said, "We've	tried and tried.	But	with	you here
4.	Pe – ter	said, "What	can I do?	You've	helped me; can
5.	Now,	like Pe – ter,	James and John,	we'll	go	fish – ing

	D		G		D/F#		
1.	all __ day long,	fish –ing all day and	fish –ing all night.
2.	com – ing a – long.	Je – sus told Pe – ter,	"Low – er your net.
3.	by __ our side,	we have caught fish both	big __ and small.
4.	I __ help you?"	Je – sus said, "Pe – ter,	wait __ and see.
5.	all __ day long;	fish –ing for peo – ple,	bring –ing them in,

	G			A	D	G/D	D	G/D	D
1.	But they did – n't	get	one	bite. _____
2.	Look and see what	you	will	get! " _____
3.	See, our nets can't	hold	them	all! " _____
4.	You'll help peo – ple	fol –	low	me." _____
5.	help – ing them to	fol –	low	him. _____

18

Once there were three friends, Peter, James and John. They were fishermen and they lived near Lake Galilee. Every day they got into their boats and went fishing. But one day, no matter how hard they tried, they couldn't catch any fish. They fished all day long, and they fished all night long, but they still didn't catch any fish. So in the morning, they sailed back to the land with their boats empty.

While they were washing out their fishing nets, they saw Jesus coming. Jesus said to Peter, "Would you row me out into the lake?" Peter said to Jesus, "Yes, if you want me to, I'll take you." So he rowed Jesus out into the lake. Then Jesus said, "Peter, put your fishing net down into the water right here." Peter said, "We fished all day long, and all night long, but we didn't catch anything. But if you want me to, I'll try again."

So Peter put the fishing net into the water. What a surprise he had! All of a sudden the net was filled with fish. There were so many fish that the net began to break. So Peter called out to James and John, "Hurry, come and help us. There are so many fish the net is breaking!" James and John jumped into a boat and went out to help. They caught so many fish that soon both boats were full!

When they got back to the land, Peter said to Jesus, "Lord, why are you doing these wonderful things for me? Don't stay with me, I'm not good enough for you." But Jesus said, "Peter, don't be afraid. From now on you will be fishing for people. I want you to help people believe in me. Come now, and follow me."

So right away, Peter, James and John left their boats and followed Jesus.

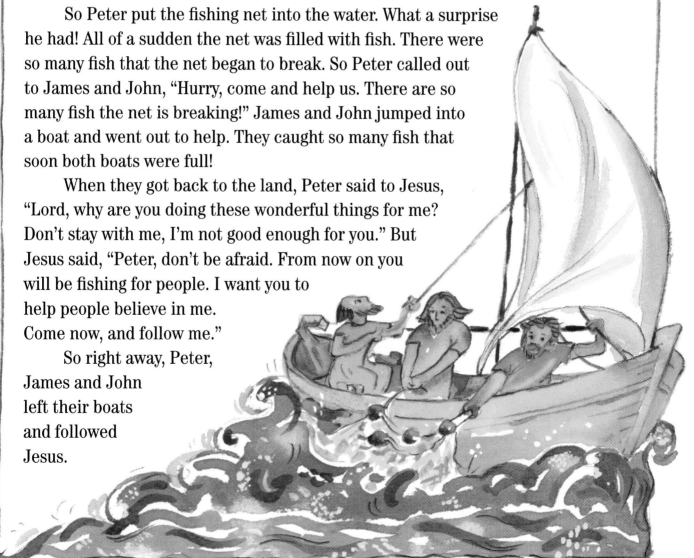

Jesus Loves The Little Children

1. Je - sus loves the lit - tle __ chil - dren, you and
2. "Come and fol - low," Je - sus __ says to you and

1. me. Je - sus loves the lit - tle __ chil - dren,
2. me. "Come and fol - low," Je - sus __ says to

1. you and me. Je - sus calls the
2. you and me. "I will bless you,"

1. lit - tle __ chil - dren, you and me.
2. Je - sus __ says to you and me.

1. Je - sus calls the lit - tle __ chil - dren, you and
2. "I will bless you," Je - sus __ says to you and

1. me.
2. me.

One day while Jesus was teaching his friends, some people came to him bringing their little children. They wanted their children to see Jesus, and they wanted Jesus to bless them. This made his friends angry. They didn't want anyone to bother Jesus while he was teaching. So they said to the people, "Keep your children away. Stop bothering Jesus."

But Jesus said, "No, don't stop them. Let the little children come to me. I love children very much and I want them near me." So the people brought their children close to Jesus.

Jesus turned to his friends and said, "If you want to go to heaven you must be just like these little children."

Then Jesus took the children in his arms and hugged them. He smiled at them and gave them his blessing.

How Much God Loves Us

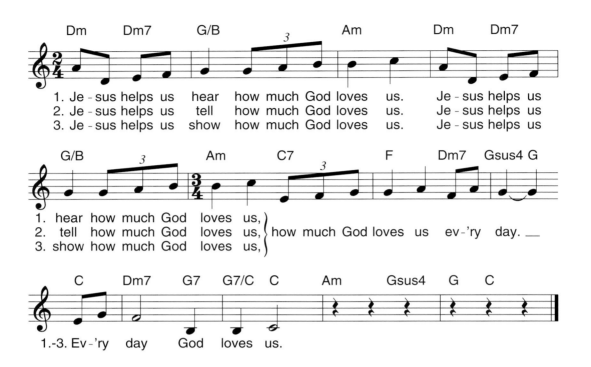

1. Je - sus helps us   hear   how much God loves   us.   Je - sus helps us
2. Je - sus helps us   tell   how much God loves   us.   Je - sus helps us
3. Je - sus helps us   show   how much God loves   us.   Je - sus helps us

1. hear how much God   loves   us, } how much God loves us   ev -'ry   day. __
2. tell how much God   loves   us, }
3. show how much God   loves   us, }

1.-3. Ev -'ry   day   God   loves   us.

Jesus wanted everyone to know about God. So he went from town to town telling people how much God loves us.

One day he was coming from a city called Tyre on his way to a place near Galilee. While Jesus was walking along, some people came to him, bringing a man who couldn't hear because he was deaf. And the poor man couldn't talk very well, either. Some of the people said to Jesus, "Please help this man. We know that if you put your hands on him he will get better. Jesus, please touch him so he will be able to hear and talk."

Jesus felt sorry for the man who couldn't hear, and wanted to help him. So he put his hands on the deaf man's ears and then he touched his tongue. Jesus looked up to heaven, and he said to the man, "Listen, listen . . . now you can hear." And suddenly the man could hear. And he could talk, too, just like everyone else!

When the people heard the man talking, they could hardly believe it! They were so excited that they ran and told all their friends, "Jesus can make deaf people hear and talk. Everything he does is so wonderful!"

Thank You, Lord

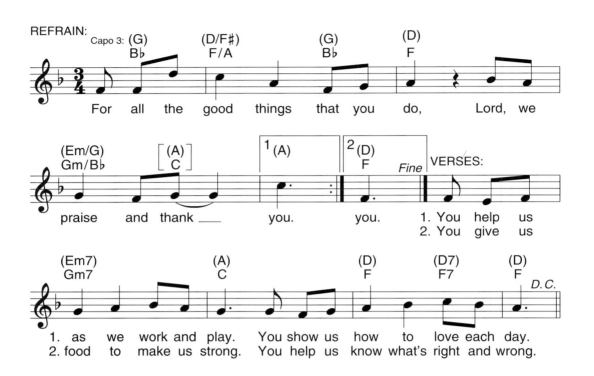

REFRAIN:

Capo 3: (G) Bb — (D/F#) F/A — (G) Bb — (D) F

For all the good things that you do, Lord, we

(Em/G) Gm/Bb — [(A) C] — 1 (A) — 2 (D) F — *Fine*   VERSES:

praise and thank ___ you. you. 1. You help us
2. You give us

(Em7) Gm7 — (A) C — (D) F — (D7) F7 — (D) F   *D.C.*

1. as we work and play. You show us how to love each day.
2. food to make us strong. You help us know what's right and wrong.

24

One day, Jesus was going to a big city called Jerusalem. On his way, he saw ten people who were very sick. They had a terrible disease called leprosy. The sores on their skin were so ugly, no one wanted to come near them. They all begged Jesus to heal them. They cried out, "Jesus, please help us get well!" And Jesus said, "Yes, I will help you." Then he said, "Now go, let the priests see you."

As they went to look for the priests, something wonderful happened to them. All of their ugly sores went away and they didn't have leprosy anymore! Jesus had healed them.

One of them was so excited that he started shouting, "Thank you, God! Thank you! Thank you!" And he ran all the way back to Jesus and knelt down in front of him and said, "Look, Jesus, I don't have those ugly sores anymore. You healed me. Thank you for making me well."

Jesus said to the man, "I healed all ten people, yet you are the only one who came back to say thank you." Then Jesus said, "Because you believe in me, I promise you that one day you will live with me in heaven."

Jesus Always Helps Us

Capo 3: (G) / Bb ... (C) / Eb ... (G) / Bb

1. Je - sus al - ways helps us when we feel a - fraid.
2. Je - sus al - ways helps us when we feel a - lone.

(Am7) / Cm7 ... (D7) / F7 ... (G) / Bb ... (C) / Eb ... (A) / C ... (D) / F

1. All we have to do is say, "Je - sus, help me ev - 'ry day."
2. All we have to do is say, "Je - sus, help me ev - 'ry day."

(G) / Bb ... (C) / Eb ... (G) / Bb

1. Je - sus al - ways helps us when we feel a - fraid.
2. Je - sus al - ways helps us when we feel a - lone.

One day Jesus went up on a mountain because he wanted to be alone with God. He stayed there all night praying.

Early the next morning, Jesus came down from the mountain to Lake Galilee. A big storm was blowing on the lake and Jesus looked and saw a boat in the middle of the storm. The wind was blowing so hard and the waves were so high that the little boat was almost sinking.

Jesus saw that his friends were in the boat and they were very frightened. So he went walking out to them on the water. When his friends saw him, they were even more frightened. They said, "Is that a ghost?" But Jesus called out, "Don't be afraid, I'm here!" Then Peter said, "Lord, if that really is you, call me to walk over to you on the water." So Jesus said, "Come on, Peter, walk over here."

So Peter got out of the boat and started walking on the water to Jesus. But the storm was still blowing very hard, and Peter got scared and started sinking into the water. He cried out to Jesus, "Lord, help me!" Jesus put out his hand and helped Peter up. Then he said to Peter, "Why were you afraid? Why didn't you believe in me? Didn't you know I would help you?"

Then Peter and Jesus got into the boat and at once the storm stopped blowing.

People Worry

One day Jesus said
to his friends:

I don't want you to worry. I don't want you to worry about anything. God will always take care of you. Look up at the sky. See all the birds flying there? They don't plant seeds. They don't grow their own food, do they? But God takes care of them and makes sure they have enough food to eat. God loves the birds. But God loves you even more than the birds. And God will always take care of you.

Look at all the flowers that grow in the field. They don't make clothes to wear. But see how pretty they are. They're much prettier than all the kings and queens of the world. Now if God takes care of the birds and the flowers, you know that God will take even better care of you because God loves you very much. So don't worry. God knows everything you need. If you believe and trust in God, God will always take care of you.

Take My Hand

REFRAIN:

D   A   Bm

Take my hand, _____ take my hand. _____ Stay with

E   1 A6   A   2 A   Asus4   A   *Fine*

me, be my friend now. friend. _____

VERSES:

Asus4/B   A/C♯   D   E   A

1. Je – sus,   Je – sus,   Je – sus, you love us.
2. Je – sus,   Je – sus,   Je – sus, you help us.

A9   D/A   Bm/A   E   *D.C.*

1.,2. Je – sus,   Je – sus,   Je – sus, you care.

One day Jesus went to visit his friend Peter. Two of his other friends, James and John, went with him. As soon as they came to Peter's house, Peter said to Jesus, "I'm so glad you're here! My wife's mother is very sick. She has a very high fever and can't get out of bed." Jesus said, "Take me to her."

When Jesus saw the woman, he went over and took her by the hand and said, "Come, get up! I have made you well."

And suddenly, her fever was gone and she wasn't sick anymore. So she got up and began to make dinner for Jesus and his friends.

The Tiny Seed

Jesus wants all his friends to know about God and how much God loves us. He wants us to know that God loves all the people in the world. No matter where we live, we are all God's family. And Jesus calls this family the Kingdom of God. Sometimes Jesus tells us stories to help us understand. One day Jesus said,

Do you know what the Kingdom of God is like? It is like a tiny, tiny mustard seed. Now a mustard seed is one of the tiniest seeds in the whole world. But when you plant it in the ground, and when you water it, it grows and grows and grows. It grows so big that it becomes one of the biggest trees in the whole world. It becomes so big that the birds come and build their nests in it.

And that's what the Kingdom of God is like. There is room for you and me and everyone.

The Money Box

C **C/E** **F** **Gm/B♭**

1. The rich came with their mon - ey. They came with
2. The wid - ow came with pen - nies. She came with
3. The wid - ow's gift was spe - cial. Her gift was

Am/C **Dm** **B♭** **C**

1. lots of mon - ey. The rich came with their
2. on - ly pen - nies. The wid - ow came with
3. ver - ry spe - cial. The wid - ow's gift was

F **C** **G7/D** **C** **G**

1. mon - ey, and put what they had, and put what they had, and
2. pen - nies, and put all she had, and put all she had, and
3. spe - cial: she put all she had, she put all she had, she

F/A **Em/G** **Dm/F** **C** **Dm7** **C** **Dm7**

1. put what they had in the ⎫
2. put all she had in the ⎬ mon - ey box, the mon - ey box, the
3. put all she had in the ⎭

C **Dm7** **C**

1.-3. mon - ey box, the mon - ey box.

34

One day Jesus was in the temple with his friends. He was teaching them and answering all their questions. While they were there, people came to the temple and put money into the money box. Many rich people came and put lots of money into the box.

Then, along came a poor woman who was a widow. Her husband had died and she didn't have very much money. She put only two pennies into the box and that was all the money she had.

When Jesus saw her put only two pennies in, he said to his friends, "Do you see that poor woman by the money box? I tell you, she put in more than all those rich people."

His friends didn't understand what he meant. So Jesus said, "The rich people gave lots of money, but they have more money than they need. But this woman is a widow and she is very poor. She put in only two pennies and it was all the money she had. So really, her gift is more special than all the others because she gave all the money she had."

We Believe

REFRAIN:

We be - lieve, Je - sus, we be - lieve in you. O

yes, we be - lieve, — Je - sus, we be - lieve — in you. —

Fine

VERSES:

1. You bring life to us. _____
2. You bring hope to us. _____

1. You bring life to us. _____
2. You bring hope to us. _____

D. C.

This is a story about how Jesus helped a little girl. She was twelve years old and her mother and father loved her very, very much. It happened this way.

One day Jesus and his friends crossed over Lake Galilee in a boat. When the people saw Jesus getting out of the boat, they gathered around him. They wanted to be with him and listen to him. While he was talking to them, a man came running up to Jesus. His name was Jairus. Jairus could hardly talk because he had been running so fast. He said, "Please come to my house. My little girl is so sick, I'm afraid she is going to die. But if you come and put your hands on her, I know she will get well. Please come with me."

So Jesus hurried off with Jairus. While they were on their way, some people came from Jairus's house and said, "Jairus, your little girl has just died. Jesus can't help her now." Jairus looked at Jesus, and Jesus said to him, "Don't worry, just believe in me. Everything will be all right." So they hurried on to Jairus' house.

When they got there, they could hear lots of people crying, because they all thought the little girl was dead. Jesus said, "Don't cry. The little girl is not dead, she is sleeping."

But the people didn't believe Jesus and they laughed at him. Jesus told the people to stay outside while he went into the house. The little girl's mother and father took Jesus to the room where she was lying in bed. Jesus went over to the little girl and held her hand. Then he said to her, "Little girl, little girl, get up."

Suddenly, the little girl opened her eyes and saw Jesus, and her mother and father. She jumped out of bed and began to walk around! The people could hardly believe their eyes when they saw that the little girl was alive and walking around.

I'm Sorry

1. When we say, "I'm sor - ry," ____
2. When we say, "I for - give you,"
3. When we say, "Let's be friends now,"

1. it is a hap - py time for ev - 'ry - bod - y, and for
2. it is a hap - py time for ev - 'ry - bod - y, and for
3. it is a hap - py time for ev - 'ry - bod - y, and for

1. you and me; when we say, "I'm sor - ry." ____
2. you and me; when we say, "I for - give you."
3. you and me; when we say, "Let's be friends now."

One day Jesus said to his friends, I want to tell you a story about a boy who left home. The boy lived on a farm with his mother and father and his older brother. The mother and father loved both of their sons very much. One day the younger son came to his father and said, "I know that someday you will give everything you have to me and my brother. But I don't want to wait. I want to leave home and live by myself. Can I have my money now?" The father didn't want his son to go because he was so young, but he said, "All right, you can have your money now."

So the boy packed his clothes and left home, and went to live in a country far, far away. He did a lot of things he shouldn't have done and he spent all of his money on silly things. Soon, he didn't have any money left. He couldn't even buy any food. He felt very sorry for himself. He was tired and hungry. And he was very lonely.

He didn't know what to do. Then one day a rich man gave him a job taking care of pigs. But the rich man didn't pay him very much money. The boy became sadder and sadder, and hungrier and hungrier. His life away from home wasn't as much fun as he thought it would be.

One day he said, "I want to go home. I want to tell my father I'm sorry. It was wrong for me to leave home and to waste all that money. Maybe my father will let me work on his farm and I will have enough to eat!" So that very day, the boy decided to go home. He didn't know what his father was going to say. But he went anyway.

While he was a long way from the house, his father looked out and saw him coming. He could hardly believe his eyes! He said, "It's my son!

My son is coming home!" He ran to meet him,
and he hugged him and kissed him.
The boy said to his father, "I'm sorry
I hurt you. Can I come home?"
His father was so happy to see him.
He said to the servants,
"Quick, bring
the best clothes and
shoes for my son. And
hurry, get a big party
ready with lots of food and
music. We're going to sing and
dance because my son went away
and has come home again. He was
lost, but now he has been found."
So they had a big party for the boy
who came home.
After Jesus told this story, he said to his
friends, God is like the father in this story.
God is always happy to have us home again.

Bartimaeus

One day Jesus and his disciples went to a town called Jericho. There was a blind man living there and his name was Bartimaeus. On the day that Jesus went to Jericho, Bartimaeus was sitting on the ground beside the road. He heard a lot of people passing by. They all sounded very excited and were making a lot of noise. Bartimaeus asked them, "What's happening? What's going on?" (Remember, Bartimaeus was blind and couldn't see.) The people said, "Jesus is here and everyone has come out to see him."

When he heard that Jesus was there, Bartimaeus cried out, "Jesus, help me!" Some of the people who were there scolded him and said, "Be quiet! Don't bother Jesus!" But Bartimaeus cried out even louder, "Jesus, help me! Please!" When Jesus heard someone calling him, he stopped and looked around and said, "Who's calling me?" One of his friends said, "It's that blind man over there." Jesus said, "Tell him to come here." So she went over to Bartimaeus and said, "Hurry, get up, Jesus wants to see you. Don't be afraid."

So Bartimaeus jumped up and she took him over to Jesus. Jesus looked right at Bartimaeus and asked him, "What do you want me to do for you?" The blind man said, "Jesus, please heal me so I can see." Jesus smiled at him and said, "Bartimaeus, because you believe in me, you will be able to see."

And as soon as Jesus said this, Bartimaeus was healed and could see. He was so happy! He said to Jesus, "Thank you, thank you for healing me. From now on, I'm going to follow you wherever you go." And from that moment, Bartimaeus followed Jesus going down the road.

The Good Shepherd

REFRAIN:

Je - sus is the Good Shep - herd, he knows his sheep and he loves them. Je - sus is the Good Shep - herd; he loves us all. _____ He loves us all.

VERSES:

Je - sus calls our name: [Sing your name; sing it again!] and we come to him run -ning and run -ning and run -ning and run -ning and run -ning and run -ning be - cause we love him. _____

44

This is a story Jesus told his friends about a shepherd and his sheep. Once there was a shepherd who had a hundred sheep. He always took very good care of them. He knew all their names and he loved them very much. Every day he took his sheep out onto the hillside where there was lots of grass for them to eat.

One day, when they were on the hillside, one of the little sheep wandered away from the shepherd and the other sheep. It wandered and wandered, and wandered so far away that it couldn't find its way home. It was really lost!

That night when the shepherd was calling his sheep to take them home, he saw that one little sheep was missing. The shepherd was very worried. So after he made sure all the other sheep were safe, he went to look for the little sheep that was lost. The shepherd looked all over the hillsides. He looked and he looked, and he called out its name, and at last he found the little lost sheep. The shepherd was very happy. And so was the little sheep. The shepherd picked up the little sheep, put it on his shoulder and carried it home.

When they got home, the shepherd said to his friends and neighbors, "Come! Let's have a party, because I have found my lost sheep and now it's back home, safe with me again."

And do you know what? Jesus says that he is our Good Shepherd and he loves us very much. And he will always take care of us, just like the shepherd in this story.

Walking Up To Jesus

REFRAIN:

So man-y peo-ple in the house with Je - sus,
(Final time:) For he was walk-ing in the house with Je - sus,

peo-ple, peo-ple, peo-ple come to see him! see him!
walk-ing, walk-ing, walk-ing up to Je - sus! Je - sus!

VERSES:

1. Four peo-ple came _____ car-ry-ing a man who
2. They went to the roof, _____ car-ry-ing the man who
3. Je - sus _ looked and said _ to the man who

1. could not walk. They tried _ and tried, but
2. could not walk. They made a hole wide to
3. could not walk: "Get _ up now. _____

1. could-n't get in-side, be-cause there were
2. put him in - side be-cause there were
3. You _ are _ healed. _ You can walk! " And

3. all at once the man jumped up, and ev-'ry-one said, "OH! "

One day Jesus went back to the town of Nazareth where he lived when he was a little boy. When the people heard that he was home, they said, "Let's go and see Jesus." But so many went that the house was full of people. It was so full that some of them had to stand outside.

Jesus was inside talking to the people and teaching them about God. While he was talking, four more people came bringing a crippled man who couldn't walk. They were carrying him on a stretcher. They wanted Jesus to help the man, but there were so many people that they couldn't get into the house.

So what do you think they did? They took the man on the stretcher and climbed up onto the roof and made a big hole in it. Then they put the man down through the hole, so that he was lying right in front of Jesus.

Jesus looked up and saw the four people looking down through the hole in the roof and he said to them, "Thank you for bringing this man to me and for believing that I can help him." Then Jesus said to the man who couldn't walk, "You can get up now, I have healed you. You can walk." And at once the man jumped up and started to walk.

Everyone was amazed to see him walking. They said, "We have never seen anything like this! Jesus is wonderful! He can do everything."

I'll Help You

Em   Bm   C

1. Once there was a man who trav – eled all a –
2. Rob – bers beat him up, who took ev – 'ry – thing he
3. Peo – ple saw the man, but would – n't stop to
4. Then there came a good man; would he stop to
5. Like the good _____ man I'll help you all I

G   C   G/B   Am6

1. lone: On the road to Jer – i – cho, the road to
2. had: On the road to Jer – i – cho, the road to
3. help: On the road to Jer – i – cho, the road to
4. help? On the road to Jer – i – cho, the road to
5. can: On the road to heav – en, the _____ road to

[last time: E   A   E]

B7   Em   B7   Em   Am   Em

1. Jer – i – cho, he trav – eled all a – lone. _____
2. Jer – i – cho, took ev – 'ry – thing he had. _____
3. Jer – i – cho, they would – n't stop to help. _____
4. Jer – i – cho, _____ yes, he stopped to help. _____
5. heav – en, I'll _____ help you all I can. _____

One day Jesus told his friends a story about a good person who helped a man who had been hurt by robbers. This is the story Jesus told them.

Once there was a man who was going from the city of Jerusalem to a town called Jericho. It was a long way from Jerusalem to Jericho and this man was all by himself. While he was walking along the road to Jericho, some robbers saw him. They said, "Look, that man is all by himself. Let's beat him up." So they ran up to him and beat him up and took everything he had. When the robbers left him, he was almost dead.

Later, a man who worked in the temple came down the road. But when he saw the man who was hurt, he just kept on walking. He didn't stop to help.

Later on, another man came by and he didn't help him either. When he saw the man who was hurt, he even went to the other side of the road so he didn't have to see the man's cuts and bruises.

Then at last a good man from Samaria came along. When he saw the man who was hurt, he felt sorry for him. He said, "That poor man is hurt, he needs help." So he went over to him and cleaned his cuts and bruises and put bandages on them. Then he put the man who was hurt up on his donkey and took him to a house where he could take care of him.

The next day the good man from Samaria said to the owner of the house, "I must go now, but here is some money. Please take good care of this man until he gets well."

After Jesus told this story, he said to his friends, "I want you to help other people just like the good man in the story."

Tell Them, Feed Them Well

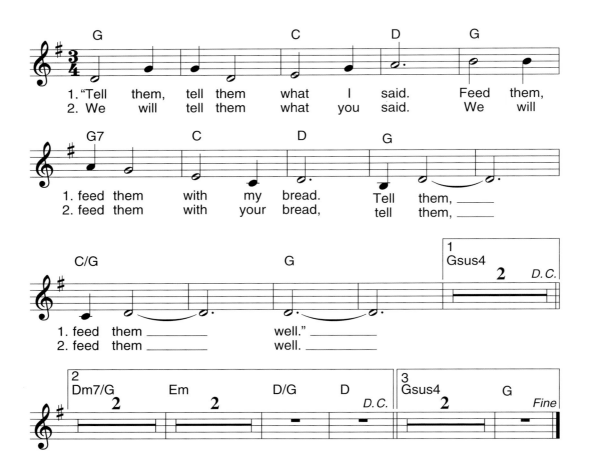

1. "Tell them, tell them what I said. Feed them,
2. We will tell them what what you said. We will

1. feed them with my bread. Tell them, _____
2. feed them with your bread, tell them, _____

1. feed them _____ well." _____
2. feed them _____ well. _____

Jesus was a wonderful teacher. Many people came from all over to listen to him.

One day, when Jesus went up a mountain with his friends, about five thousand people followed them. (That's a lot of people, isn't it?) They wanted to hear what Jesus was teaching his friends. They stayed there so long listening to Jesus that it got very late and the people were getting hungry. So his friends said to Jesus, "Where are we going to get enough food for all these people? It's late and they're hungry."

Jesus said, "How much food do we have with us?" His friend Andrew answered, "Here's a little boy who has five loaves of bread and two fish, but that won't be enough to feed all these people." Jesus said, "Tell them all to sit down on the grass."

So everyone sat down and waited to see what Jesus was going to do. Then Jesus asked the little boy, "Will you give me your bread and fish?" The little boy said, "Yes, you can have them." And he gave Jesus his five loaves of bread and two fish.

Jesus took the bread and fish, said a prayer of thanks to God, and said to his friends, "Take this food and give it to the people to eat." So they did. And do you know what happened? There was enough bread for everyone. There was so much food, that even after the people had eaten all they could, there was still lots of bread left over.

When the people saw what Jesus had done, they said, "Jesus does wonderful things! He really is the Son of God."

Zacchaeus

Once there was a short man whose name was Zacchaeus. He lived in a town called Jericho. Zacchaeus was a bad tax collector. A lot of people didn't like him because he didn't treat people fairly. He cheated them out of their money and kept it for himself. The people said that Zacchaeus was a sinner. And it was true. But then something very special happened to Zacchaeus. It happened like this:

One day Jesus and his friends came to Jericho. Everyone in the town was very excited because they heard that Jesus was coming. Soon a big crowd gathered to see him. Zacchaeus was there, too. But he couldn't see anything because the crowd was so big, and Zacchaeus was a very, very short man. Everyone around him seemed so tall. No matter where he went, he couldn't see Jesus. So what do you think he did? He said, "I'll climb up into this sycamore tree. Then I'll be able to see Jesus." So Zacchaeus climbed up the sycamore tree and he could see everything. There he was, sitting way up in the tree when Jesus passed right below him.

Then a wonderful thing happened! Jesus looked right up at Zacchaeus. And he called up to him, "Zacchaeus, hurry! Come down! I want to come and stay with you at your house." Zacchaeus could hardly believe it. "Jesus wants to see me!" He climbed down out of that sycamore tree as fast as he could. And there he was, standing right in front of Jesus!

This made some of the people very angry. They said, "Look, Jesus is going to stay with that sinner, Zacchaeus. He doesn't deserve to be with Jesus. He's a cheat!" Zacchaeus said to Jesus, "They're right. I have cheated people out of money. I have done a lot of bad things. But now that I have met you, Jesus, I am going to give back all that money. And from now on, I'm going to share everything I have with poor people."

Jesus smiled at Zacchaeus, and said, "Zacchaeus, I want to stay with you. I came to help people just like you; people who do bad things, but who want to change and do good things. And I promise you, one day you will come and stay with me in heaven."

Jesus, I Will Stay With You

REFRAIN:

Capo 3: (Em) / Gm ... (Am7) / Cm7 ... (D7) / F7

Je - sus, I will stay with you, close to you,

(B) / D ... (C) / E♭ ... (Am7) / Cm7

Je - sus. I will al - ways stay with you,

(D7) / F7 ... (Esus4) / Gsus4 ... (Em) / Gm *Fine*

VERSES:

(C) / E♭

close to you, Je - sus.

1. Just like Mar - y,
2. All I have I
3. Bless my friends and

(D) / F ... (Em) / Gm ... (Am) / Cm ... (Bsus4) / Dsus4 ... (B) / D *D.C.*

1. I will stay here be - side you, ev - 'ry day.
2. give to you. Help me, Lord, in all I do.
3. fam - i - ly. Bless them all, as you bless me.

56

Jesus always tried to help people. He helped people who were sick and people who were sad. He healed people and taught them how to love each other and how to love God. But even though Jesus did all these wonderful things, some people hated him. The leaders told lies about him and wanted Jesus to be killed.

So they took him to Pontius Pilate who was the ruler of the people. Pilate asked Jesus many questions but he couldn't find anything Jesus did that was wrong. So he said to the people, "This man, Jesus, hasn't done anything wrong. I'm going to let him go." But the people shouted, "Kill him! Kill him!" Pilate said, "Why? Isn't he your king? Do you want me to kill your king?"

The people shouted even louder, "No, he's not our king, kill him, kill him!" Some of Pilate's soldiers dressed Jesus up to look like a king. They even made a crown out of sharp thorns and they put it on his head. They laughed at him and they hit him with a stick. Then they took Jesus back to Pilate. Pilate said to the people, "If you want Jesus killed, you kill him yourselves."

So the people made a cross out of wood and made Jesus carry it up a long hill. When they got to the top of the hill, the soldiers nailed Jesus to the cross. His mother Mary was there with him and so was his friend John. They loved Jesus and wanted to stay near him. Other people were there making fun of him. Jesus asked God to forgive the people who were killing him. He prayed, "Forgive these people, they don't know what they are doing."

After three long hours on the cross, Jesus died. One of the soldiers who watched him die said, "Jesus was a good man."

Later, the friends of Jesus came and took him off the cross and put him in a tomb. They all went away feeling very sad.

Jesus Lives!

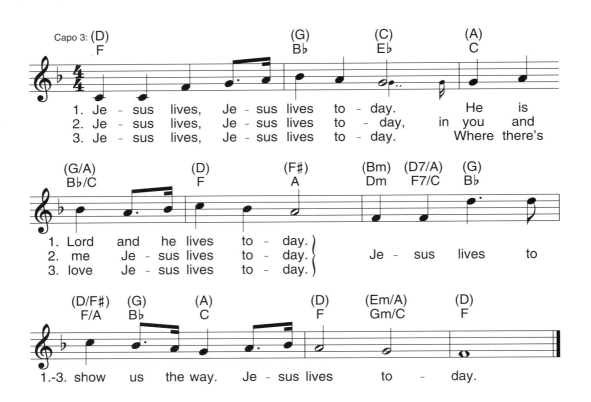

Capo 3: (D) F

1. Je - sus lives, Je - sus lives to - day. He is
2. Je - sus lives, Je - sus lives to - day, in you and
3. Je - sus lives, Je - sus lives to - day. Where there's

1. Lord and he lives to - day.
2. me Je - sus lives to - day.
3. love Je - sus lives to - day.
Je - sus lives to

1.-3. show us the way. Je - sus lives to - day.

Do you remember the story of how Jesus died? How some people hated him, and hurt him and then nailed him to a cross and killed him? After Jesus died, some of his friends took him down off the cross and put him in a tomb. They rolled a great big stone in front of the tomb. Mary, his mother, and his friends went home very sad because Jesus had died and they wouldn't see him anymore.

Then on Sunday a wonderful thing happened. Some of Jesus' friends woke up early, and they said, "Let's go to the tomb where Jesus is." They wanted to put special oil on the body of Jesus. So, early on Sunday morning, just after the sun came up, Joanna, Mary Magdalen and some other women went to the tomb where Jesus had been buried.

On the way, they said to each other, "How will we move that big stone away from the tomb? Who will help us?" And what do you think they saw when they got there? They saw that the big stone had already been rolled away and Jesus wasn't in the tomb any more. The tomb was empty.

The women didn't know what to think. They were very excited, but they were a little frightened, too. And then suddenly

they saw a young man wearing dazzling white clothes sitting beside the tomb. Now they were really frightened. But the young man said, "Don't be afraid. I know you came here looking for Jesus who died on the cross. But he is not here. He is alive! Now go, tell his friends he is alive and is coming to see them." So Joanna, Mary Magdalen and the other women hurried off.

As they were running back to tell the others what had happened, Jesus met them. He called out to them, "Peace be with you. Don't be afraid."

The women stopped and said, "Can this really be Jesus?" Then Jesus said to them, "Yes, I am Jesus. I really am alive."

The women were so happy to see Jesus, that they ran to him and hugged him. Then Jesus said, "Hurry, tell my friends I am alive and they will see me, too." So the women ran off to tell the others the good news that Jesus is alive!

Christopher Walker, internationally-known lecturer, composer and conductor, was born and educated in England, attending Bristol University where he earned his degree. He served as Director of Music at Clifton Cathedral in Bristol and Director of Music for the Clifton Diocese.

Christopher is presently residing in Los Angeles where he is combining the roles of music lecturer at Mount St. Mary's College and musician for the Family/RCIA Sunday Mass at St. Paul the Apostle Church. Christopher is also a member of the North American Forum on the Catechumenate.

Christopher's compositons have been published in the St. Thomas More Group collections: *Sing Of The Lord's Goodness; We Are Your People; Lead Me, O Lord; Come To Set Us Free;* and *Holy Is God.* His own published works are *Music For Children's Liturgy Of The Word, Out Of Darkness, Calling The Children* and latest release, *Christ Is Here.*

Paule Freeburg, DC, is Religion Consultant for the Diocese of San Jose, CA. With a degree in Speech and Hearing and a graduate degree in Theology, she has an extensive background working in Religious Education with both children and adults. Paule has taught elementary and high school; she has served as Director of Religious Education and has directed Sacramental programs for children; she has directed parish RCIA programs and presented RCIA institutes in the USA and England.

Paule currently works in Development and Public Relations at a school for economically disadvantaged children. She presents workshops around the USA on the Spirituality of Children and Celebrating the Word with Children. She is primary author of the biblical material for *Sunday,* a Liturgy of the Word for Children series, and is co-author of *A Child Shall Lead Them* (Treehaus Communications, Inc.).

Jean Germano is a graduate of FIT in New York City. She worked as an illustrator in New York before relocating to Rome, Italy. There she worked for the North American College as well as the Bishops' Office for Visitors. After spending fifteen years in Rome, Jean moved with her husband and two children to Portland, Oregon. She began doing freelance art for Oregon Catholic Press and in 1986 became their Art Director.

Jean dedicates the art in this book to all God's children, but most of all to her children, Christopher and Diana.